Y0-BVX-509

ALL-AUDIO
ITALIAN
BASIC–INTERMEDIATE

Want to take your

Italian further?

Living Language® makes it easy with a wide range of programs that will suit your particular needs.

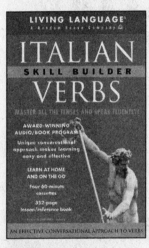

An award-winning program that will help you master verbs—the key to fluency. This is not just a book full of verb charts, but a program that teaches you how to *use* verbs. There's also a handy grammar summary for easy reference. 40 lessons on four 60-minute cassettes, plus a 352-page coursebook.

Skill Builder: Italian Verbs
ISBN: 0-609-60441-4   **$29.95/C$42.00**

ISBN: 0-609-80427-8 (Coursebook Only) $6.95/C$9.50

Available at your local bookstore or by calling **1-800-733-3000**
For a complete list of Living Language titles, please visit our
Web site at **www.livinglanguage.com**

LIVING LANGUAGE®
A Random House Company

ALL-AUDIO
ITALIAN
BASIC–INTERMEDIATE

Lisa Ferrante

Based on *Italian All the Way*
By S. Bancheri and M. Lettieri

LIVING LANGUAGE®
A Random House Company

Copyright © 1997, 1999 by Living Language, A Random House Company

All rights reserved under Pan-American Copyright Pages. No part of this book may
be reproduced or transmitted in any form or by any means, electronic or mechanical,
including photocopying, recording, or by any information storage and
retrieval system, without permission in writing from the publisher.

Published by Living Language, A Random House Company, New York, New York.
Living Language is a member of the Random House Information Group.

Living Language and colophon are registered trademarks of Random House, Inc.

Library of Congress Cataloging-in-Publication Data available.

Designed by Sophie Chin

www.livinglanguage.com

Part of boxed set ISBN 978-0-307-29120-2

This 2007 edition printed in the United States of America.

10 9 8 7 6 5 4 3 2 1

ACKNOWLEDGMENTS

Thanks to the Living Language team:
Lisa Alpert, Elizabeth Bennett, Christopher Warnasch,
Zviezdana Verzich, Suzanne McQuade,
Helen Tang, Denise DeGennaro, Pat Ehresmann,
Linda Schmidt, Lisa Montebello,
Marina Padakis, and Sophie Chin.

FREE ACCESS TO MORE
PRACTICE ONLINE

Would you like to enhance your All-Audio
learning with extra practice online?
Go to *www.livinglanguage.com/bonus/allaudio/italian*
for bonus exercises, grammar review, and culture notes!

How to Use this Course

This course was designed using an all-audio method that emphasizes spoken communication and, at the same time, gives you the flexibility of learning Italian wherever and whenever you'd like. However, if you prefer to see the course material written, we've also included this booklet for your benefit as a reference tool. After you have completed each lesson, you can go back and review the words you learned, or listen to the dialogue again with the text to help you recognize the spellings and constructions of specific words and sentences. Please note that this booklet is not a full or a direct transcript of the recordings: for example, the dialogue appears first in each lesson of the booklet, but will not be the first thing you hear on the recordings. We hope you enjoy learning Italian with our book-free, all-audio method, but hope that you will also take advantage of this booklet to help advance your Italian skills if you prefer to do so.

CONTENTS

DIALOGUES AND NEW VOCABULARY 1

Lesson 1: Greetings and Introductions 1

Lesson 2: Snack Time 4

Lesson 3: At the Airport 6

Lesson 4: Nationalities 8

Lesson 5: Plans for the Weekend 10

Lesson 6: Clothing 12

Lesson 7: Studies 14

Lesson 8: On the Telephone 16

Lesson 9: Months, Seasons, Dates,
  and Weather 18

Lesson 10: The Family 20

Lesson 11: Food and Drink 23

Lesson 12: A Typical Day 26

Lesson 13: Asking for and Giving Directions .. 28

Lesson 14: Radio and Television 30

Lesson 15: Traveling by Train 32

Lesson 16: In a Hotel 34

Lesson 17: A Tour in Italy 36

Lesson 18: A Job Interview 38

Lesson 19: Sports 40

Lesson 20: The Home 42

Lesson 21: Newspapers 44

Lesson 22: At the Bank 46

Lesson 23: The Post Office 48

Lesson 24: Health 50

Lesson 25: Computers and the Internet 52

Lesson 26: To the Opera 54

Lesson 27: Music 56

Lesson 28: Fruits and Vegetables 58

Lesson 29: At the Supermarket 60

Lesson 30: At the Tobacco Store 62
Lesson 31: Hair 64
Lesson 32: Money 66
Lesson 33: Renting a Car 68
Lesson 34: In a Shoe Store 70
Lesson 35: A Tour of the City 72

GRAMMAR SUMMARY 75

Subject Pronouns 75
Emphatic Pronouns 75
Reflexive Pronouns 75
Direct Object Pronouns 75
Indirect Object Pronouns 75
Double Object Pronouns 75
Plural of Nouns and Adjectives 76
Indefinite Articles (*a, an*) 76
Definite Article (*the*) 76
Prepositions + Definite Articles 76
Demonstrative Pronouns 76
Demonstrative Adjectives 76
Possessive Adjectives 77
Comparatives 77
Irregular Comparatives and Superlatives 77
The Adjective *bello* (beautiful) 78
The Adjective *buono* (good) 78
Double Negatives 78
Regular Verbs Ending in *–are* 79
Regular Verbs Ending in *–ere* 80
Regular Verbs Ending in *–ire* 81

GLOSSARY OF GRAMMATICAL TERMS 82

ALL-AUDIO
ITALIAN
BASIC–INTERMEDIATE

LESSON 1
SALUTI E PRESENTAZIONI
Greetings and Introductions

1.

Signor Rossi:	Buon giorno, signorina Smith, come sta?
Signorina Smith:	Bene, grazie. E Lei?
Signor Rossi:	Molto bene.
Signorina Smith:	Signor Rossi, Le presento la signora Wilson.
Signor Rossi:	Piacere, sono Giorgio Rossi.

Mr. Rossi:	*Good morning, Miss Smith, how are you?*
Miss Smith:	*Fine, thank you. And you?*
Mr. Rossi:	*Very well.*
Miss Smith:	*Mr. Rossi, I'd like you to meet Mrs. Wilson.*
Mr. Rossi:	*Pleased to meet you, I am Giorgio Rossi.*

2.

Roberto:	Ciao, Jane. Come stai?
Jane:	Sto bene, grazie. E tu?
Roberto:	Molto bene.
Jane:	Roberto, ti presento Carol.
Roberto:	Molto lieto, Carol. Mi chiamo Roberto.

Roberto:	*Hi, Jane. How are you?*
Jane:	*I'm fine, thanks. And you?*
Roberto:	*Very well.*
Jane:	*Roberto, I'd like you too meet Carol.*
Roberto:	*Pleased to meet you, Carol. My name is Roberto.*

NEW VOCABULARY*

abbastanza bene	*rather well*
A domani.	*See you tomorrow.*
A più tardi.	*See you later.*
A presto.	*See you later.*
Arrivederci.	*See you later.*
ArrivederLa.	*Good-bye. (fml)*
bene	*fine; well*
benissimo/a	*very well*
Buon giorno.	*Hello.; Good morning/ afternoon.*
Buona sera.	*Good evening.*
Ciao.	*Hi.; Bye.*
Come si chiama Lei?	*What is your name? (fml)*
Come ti chiami?	*What is your name? (infml)*
Come sta?	*How are you? (fml)*
Come stai?	*How are you? (infml)*
così così	*so-so*
E Lei?	*And you? (fml)*
essere	*to be*
E tu?	*And you? (infml)*
Grazie.	*Thank you.*
io	*I*
Lei	*you (fml); she*
Le presento . . .	*I'd like you to meet . . . (fml)*
loro	*they; them*
lui	*he*
male (adv)	*bad*
Mi chiamo . . .	*My name is . . .*
molto bene	*very well*
noi	*we*
non	*not*
non c'è male	*not bad*
Piacere.	*Pleased to meet you.*

* The abbreviations used in the New Vocabulary lists are: *m* for "masculine"; *f* for "feminine"; *sg* for "singular"; *pl* for "plural"; *fml* for "formal usage"; *infml.* for "informal usage."

Prego.	You're welcome.
Signora	Madame; Mrs.
Signor(e)	Sir; Mr.
Signorina	Miss
Sono . . .	I'm . . .
Ti presento . . .	I'd like you to meet . . . (infml)
tu	you (infml)
voi	you (pl)

LESSON 2
UNO SPUNTINO
Snack Time

Barista:	Desiderano?
Cliente:	Qualcosa da mangiare . . . . Un panino al formaggio, una pizzetta e due tramezzini.
Barista:	Qualcosa da bere?
Cliente:	Due aranciate e due bicchieri d'acqua minerale, per piacere. Quant'è?
Barista:	Nove euro.
Cliente:	Tenga pure il resto.

Bartender:	*May I help you?*
Client:	*Something to eat . . . . A cheese sandwich, a small pizza, and two club sandwiches.*
Bartender:	*Something to drink?*
Client:	*Two orange drinks and two glasses of mineral water, please. How much is it?*
Bartender:	*Nine euros.*
Client:	*Keep the change.*

NEW VOCABULARY

acqua	*water*
acqua minerale	*mineral water*
aranciata	*orange drink*
bar (m)	*café*
bere	*to drink*
bicchiere (m)	*glass*
caffè (m)	*coffee; café*
caffelatte (m)	*coffee with milk*
cameriere/a	*waiter*
cinque	*five*
Desidera?/	*May I help you?*
Desiderano? (sg/pl)	
dieci	*ten*
due	*two*
formaggio	*cheese*
gelato	*ice cream*
limonata	*lemonade*
mangiare	*to eat*
nove	*nine*
otto	*eight*
panino	*sandwich*
pasta	*pastry*
per favore	*please*
per piacere	*please*
pizzetta	*small pizza*
qualcosa	*something*
Quant'è?	*How much is it?*
quattro	*four*
resto	*change*
sei	*six*
sette	*seven*
spuntino	*snack*
succo di frutta	*fruit juice*
tè (m)	*tea*
tramezzino	*club sandwich*
tre	*three*
uno	*one*
zero	*zero*

LESSON 3
ALL'AEROPORTO
At the Airport

Impegiata:	Il biglietto e il passaporto, per piacere. Ha bagagli?
Passeggero:	Sì, ho due valigie e una borsa a mano.
Impegiata:	Fumatori o non fumatori?
Passeggero:	Non fumatori. E un posto vicino al finestrino, per piacere.
Impegiata:	Il posto 14A è vicino al finestrino. Ecco il biglietto, il passaporto e la carta d'imbarco.

Airline Agent:	Your ticket and your passport, please. Do you have any luggage?
Passenger:	Yes, I have two suitcases and one carry-on bag.
Airline Agent:	Smoking or non-smoking?
Passenger:	Non-smoking. And a window seat, please.
Airline Agent:	Seat 14A is a window seat. Here is your ticket, your passport, and your boarding pass.

NEW VOCABULARY

aereo	airplane
aeroporto	airport
arrivo	arrival
assistente di volo (m/f)	flight attendant
avere	to have
bagagli	luggage
banco d'accettazione	check-in counter
biglietto	ticket
borsa	bag
borsa a mano	carry-on bag
Buon viaggio!	Have a nice trip!
carta d'imbarco	boarding pass
C'è . . .	There is . . .
cintura	seat belt
ci sono	there are
corridoio	aisle
diciannove	nineteen
diciassette	seventeen
diciotto	eighteen
dodici	twelve
Ecco . . .	Here is . . . /Here are . . .
facchino	porter
finestrino	window
fumatori	smoking
impiegato	employee
partenza	departure
passaporto	passport
posto	seat
prenotazione (f)	reservation
quattordici	fourteen
quindici	fifteen
sala d'aspetto	waiting room
sedici	sixteen
tredici	thirteen
undici	eleven
uscita	gate
valigia	suitcase
venti	twenty
volo	flight

LESSON 4
LE NAZIONALITÀ
Nationalities

Roberto: Sei americana?
Susan: Sì, sono di New York. E tu, sei italiano?
Roberto: No, sono spagnolo.
Susan: Lavori in Italia?
Roberto: No, non lavoro, sono studente.

Roberto: *Are you American?*
Susan: *Yes, I am from New York. And you, are you Italian?*
Roberto: *No, I am Spanish.*
Susan: *Do you work in Italy?*
Roberto: *No, I don't work, I am a student.*

NEW VOCABULARY

abitare	*to live*
americano/a	*American*
aspettare	*to wait for*
Cina	*China*
cinese	*Chinese*
di	*from*
dove	*where*
Francia	*France*
francese	*French*
frequentare	*to attend*
Germania	*Germany*
tedesco/a	*German*
Giappone	*Japan*
giapponese	*Japanese*
India	*India*
indiano/a	*Indian*
Inghilterra	*England*
inglese	*English*
insegnare	*to teach*
Italia	*Italy*
italiano/a	*Italian*
lavorare	*to work*
Messico	*Mexico*
messicano/a	*Mexican*
parlare	*to speak*
Russia	*Russia*
russo/a	*Russian*
Spagna	*Spain*
spagnolo/a	*Spanish*
Stati Uniti	*United States*
studente (m)	*student*
studentessa (f)	*student*
studiare	*to study*

LESSON 5
PROGETTI PER IL WEEK-END
Plans for the Weekend

Barbara:	Che cosa fai questo week-end?
Renzo:	Venerdì vado a Roma . . . vado da Sandra. E tu, come passi il week-end?
Barbara:	Sabato faccio una passeggiata in centro, e vado al cinema alle otto.
Renzo:	Che film danno?
Barbara:	Danno un film di Tornatore.

Barbara:	*What are you doing this weekend?*
Renzo:	*Friday I am going to Rome . . . I am going to Sandra. And you, how are you going to spend your weekend?*
Barbara:	*Saturday I am going for a walk downtown, and I'm going to the movies at eight o'clock.*
Renzo:	*What film are they showing?*
Barbara:	*They're showing a film by Tornatore.*

NEW VOCABULARY

andare	to go
cento	one hundred
Che cosa fai?	What are you doing?
cinema	movie theater
cinquanta	fifty
dare	to give
domenica	Sunday
festa	party
film (m)	movie
giorno	day
giovedì	Thursday
lunedì	Monday
martedì	Tuesday
mattina	morning
mercoledì	Wednesday
mezzanotte	midnight
mezzogiorno	noon
novanta	ninety
oggi	today
ottanta	eighty
passeggiata	(a) walk
pomeriggio	afternoon
quando	when
quaranta	forty
sabato	Saturday
sera	evening
sessanta	sixty
settanta	seventy
trenta	thirty
venerdì	Friday

LESSON 6
ABBIGLIAMENTO
Clothing

Sandra:	Quella camicia bianca è molto bella.
Daniela:	Sì, è una bella camicia.
Sandra:	Entriamo!
Sandra:	Vorrei vedere la camicia in vetrina.
Commesso:	Vuole provare questa rosa o questa gialla?
Sandra:	Provo la bianca. Se hanno la mia taglia, compro anche quell'abito.

Sandra:	*That white blouse is very beautiful.*
Daniela:	*Yes, it's a beautiful blouse.*
Sandra:	*Let's go in!*
Sandra:	*I'd like to see the blouse in the window.*
Salesman:	*Would you like to try this pink one or this yellow one?*
Sandra:	*I'll try the white one. If they have my size, I'll also buy that outfit.*

NEW VOCABULARY

abito	*outfit*
bello/a	*beautiful*
bianco/a	*white*
blu (m/f)	*blue*
camicia	*blouse*
cappello	*hat*
caro/a	*expensive*
commesso/a	*clerk; salesperson*
comprare	*to buy*
costare	*to cost*
cravatta	*tie*
entrare	*to enter*
giacca	*jacket*
giallo/a	*yellow*
gonna	*skirt*
guanti	*gloves*
magazzino	*department store*
maglione (m)	*pullover*
marrone	*brown*
mercato	*open-air market*
nero/a	*black*
pantaloni	*pants*
portare	*to wear*
prezzo	*price*
provare	*to try*
quelli/e	*those*
quello/a	*that*
questi/e	*these*
questo/a	*this*
rosa	*pink*
rosso/a	*red*
stretto/a	*tight*
taglia	*size*
vedere	*to see*
verde	*green*
vestito	*suit; dress*
vetrina	*store window*
Vorrei . . .	*I'd like . . .*

LESSON 7
GLI STUDI
Studies

Antonio:	I ragazzi vanno a scuola.
Ester:	Giovanni va già all'università, vero?
Antonio:	Sì, fa il primo anno. Studia a Roma. Deve sempre studiare.
Ester:	Anche Silvana studia sempre, legge sempre, scrive sempre. L'ultimo anno di liceo è sempre difficile.

Antonio:	*The children go to school.*
Ester:	*Giovanni is already attending university, right?*
Antonio:	*Yes, he is in his first year. He studies in Rome. He always has to study.*
Ester:	*Silvana is always studying as well, always reading, always writing. The last year of liceo is always hard.*

NEW VOCABULARY

anche	also
anno	year
classe (f)	class
corso	course
difficile	difficult
dovere	to have to
esame (m)	exam
già	already
insegnante (m/f)	teacher
leggere	to read
libro	book
matematica	math
penna	pen
potere	to be able to
prendere appunti	to take notes
primo/a	first
professore (m)	professor
professoressa (f)	professor
quaderno	notebook
ragazza	girl
ragazzo	boy
ripetere	to repeat
saggio	essay
scienza	science
scrivere	to write
scuola	school
scuola elementare	elementary school
scuola materna	nursery school
scuola media	junior high school
scuola superiore	high school
sempre	always
spiegare	to explain
storia	history
ultimo/a	last
università	university
volere	to want

LESSON 8
AL TELEFONO
On the Telephone

1.

Michele: Vorrei telefonare a New York, per
                favore. Il prefisso è due-uno-due; il
                numero è sei-due-otto-quindici-ventotto.
Centralinista: Resti in linea . . . mi dispiace, la linea è
                occupata.
Michele: Va bene, richiamo più tardi.

Michele: *I'd like to make a call to New York,*
                please. The area code is two-one-two.
                The number is six-two-eight-fifteen-twenty-
                eight.
Operator: *Hold on . . . I'm sorry, the line is busy.*
Michele: *Okay, I'll call again later.*

2.

Maria: Pronto, chi parla?
Michele: Sono Michele. Sono in una cabina
                telefonica.
Maria: Non sento bene, e non capisco quello
                che dici.
Michele: Chiudiamo!

Maria: *Hello! Who's speaking?*
Michele: *It's Michele. I am at a phone booth.*
Maria: *I can't hear well, and I don't understand*
                what you are saying.
Michele: *Let's hang up!*

NEW VOCABULARY

cabina telefonica	*telephone booth*
capire	*to understand*
carta telefonica	*telephone card*
centralino	*operator*
chiudere	*to close; to hang up*
con	*with*
dire	*to say*
dormire	*to sleep*
elenco telefonico	*telephone book*
fare una telefonata	*to make a telephone call*
finire	*to finish*
gettone (m)	*token*
linea	*line*
messaggio	*message*
mi dispiace	*I'm sorry*
numero di telefono	*telephone number*
occupato/a	*busy*
offrire	*to offer*
partire	*to leave*
più tardi	*later*
preferire	*to prefer*
prefisso	*area code*
Pronto?	*Hello?*
richiamare	*to call back*
sentire	*to hear*
telefonare	*to make a telephone call*

LESSON 9
MESI, STAGIONI, DATE E TEMPO
Months, Seasons, Dates, and Weather

Signora Rossi:	Che bella giornata!
Signor Rossi:	Ma quanti ne abbiamo oggi?
Signora Rossi:	È già il primo luglio.
Signor Rossi:	A luglio e agosto fa molto caldo. Ci sono molti turisti.
Signora Rossi:	Non capisco, preferisci quando fa freddo e piove sempre?
Signor Rossi:	Si, perchè posso stare solo.

Mrs. Rossi:	What a beautiful day!
Mr. Rossi:	But what's today's date?
Mrs. Rossi:	It's already the first of July.
Mr. Rossi:	In July and August it's very hot. There are a lot of tourists.
Mrs. Rossi:	I don't understand, do you prefer when it's cold and raining all the time?
Mr. Rossi:	Yes, because I can be alone.

NEW VOCABULARY

agosto	*August*
aprile	*April*
autunno	*fall*
data	*date*
dicembre	*December*
estate	*summer*
Fa caldo.	*It's hot.*
Fa freddo.	*It's cold.*
fare	*to do; to make*
febbraio	*February*
gennaio	*January*
giornata	*day*
giugno	*June*
inverno	*winter*
luglio	*July*
maggio	*May*
marzo	*March*
molto	*very; many*
nevicare	*to snow*
novembre	*November*
ottobre	*October*
persona	*person*
piovere	*to rain*
poco	*few*
primavera	*spring*
settembre	*September*
solo/a	*alone*
spesso	*often*
spiaggia	*beach*
stare	*to stay*
Tira vento.	*It's windy.*
turista (m/f)	*tourist*

LESSON 10
LA FAMIGLIA
The Family

Matteo:	Ho fretta. Devo comprare un regalo per mio nonno. Oggi è il suo compleanno.
Monica:	Quanti anni ha tuo nonno?
Matteo:	Ha ottant'anni.
Monica:	Alla festa vengono tutti i tuoi parenti?
Matteo:	Sì, viene tutta la mia famiglia: mia sorella, mio fratello e tutti i nostri zii e cugini.
Monica:	Beh, ciao e buon compleanno a tuo nonno!

Matteo:	*I'm in a hurry. I have to buy a gift for my grandfather. Today is his birthday.*
Monica:	*How old is your grandfather?*
Matteo:	*He's eighty.*
Monica:	*Are all of your relatives coming to the party?*
Matteo:	*Yes, my whole family is coming: my sister, my brother, and all our uncles and cousins.*
Monica:	*Well, good-bye and happy birthday to your grandfather!*

NEW VOCABULARY

avere bisogno di	to need
avere fretta	to be in a hurry
avere paura	to be afraid
avere ragione	to be right
avere torto	to be wrong
avere voglia di	to feel like
Buon compleanno!	Happy birthday!
Buon onomastico!	Happy name day!
cognata	sister-in-law
cognato	brother-in-law
compleanno	birthday
cugino	cousin
famiglia	family
fidanzato/a	fiancé(e)
figlia	daughter
figlio	son
fratello	brother
genero	son-in-law
genitori	parents
loro	their; them
madre	mother
Mamma	Mom
marito	husband
mio/a	my
moglie	wife
nipote (m/f)	grandchild; nephew; niece
nonna	grandmother
nonno	grandfather
nostro/a	our
nuora	daughter-in-law
onomastico	name day
padre (m)	father
papà (m)	dad
parenti (m pl)	relatives
regalo	gift
sorella	sister

suo/a	*his; her; your (fml)*
suocera	*mother-in-law*
suocero	*father-in-law*
Tanti auguri!	*Best wishes!*
tuo	*your (infml)*
venire	*to come*
vostro	*your (pl)*
zia	*aunt*
zio	*uncle*

LESSON 11
MANGIARE E BERE
Food and Drink

Cameriera:	Desiderate ordinare adesso?
Signora Smith:	Sì, abbiamo fame. Io vorrei del pesce ai ferri.
Signor Smith:	Io vorrei una bistecca, per favore.
Cameriera:	E per contorno?
Signor Smith:	Per me, un po' di verdura e delle patate fritte.
Signora Smith:	E io vorrei dell'insalata.
Cameriera:	E da bere, del vino?
Signor Smith:	Niente vino, una bottiglia d'acqua minerale.
Signora Smith:	E dopo un dolce.
Waitress:	Would you like to order now?
Mrs. Smith:	Yes, we are hungry. I'd like some grilled fish.
Mr. Smith:	I would like a steak, please.
Waitress:	And as a side dish?
Mr. Smith:	For me, some vegetables and some french fries.
Mrs. Smith:	And I would like some salad.
Waitress:	And to drink, some wine?
Mr. Smith:	No wine, a bottle of mineral water.
Mrs. Smith:	And later, some dessert.

NEW VOCABULARY

adesso	*now*
ai ferri	*grilled*
avere caldo	*to be hot*
avere fame	*to be hungry*
avere freddo	*to be cold*
avere sete	*to be thirsty*
avere sonno	*to be tired*
bistecca	*steak*
Buon appetito!	*Enjoy your meal!*
carne (f)	*meat*
cenare	*to have dinner*
conto	*check*
contorno	*side dish*
coperto	*cover charge*
cucchiaio	*spoon*
dolce (m)	*dessert*
forchetta	*fork*
insalata	*salad*
mai	*never*
mancia	*tip*
menù	*menu*
minestra	*soup*
nè . . . nè	*neither . . . nor*
nessuno/a	*no one*
niente	*nothing*
non . . . ancora	*not yet*
non . . . più	*no longer*
nulla	*nothing*
ordinare	*to order*
patate fritte	*french fries*
pesce	*fish*
piatto	*plate*
pollo	*chicken*
ristorante	*restaurant*
rosticceria	*rotisserie*
servizio	*service charge*

tavola calda	*hot buffet*
tavolo	*table*
tovagliolo	*napkin*
trattoria	*restaurant*
verdura	*vegetables*
vino	*wine*
vitello	*veal*

LESSON 12
UNA GIORNATA TIPICA
A Typical Day

Carla: Finalmente ci incontriamo! Ma tu sei sempre occupato?

Luigi: Sempre occupato, sempre al lavoro.

Carla: Anch'io, sai. La mattina mi sveglio alle sei, mi lavo e faccio colazione in fretta. E tu come stai?

Luigi: Sono stanco. Io non ho mai un momento per divertirmi.

Carla: Ma tu almeno hai un bel posto!

Carla: *Finally we meet! But are you always busy?*

Luigi: *Always busy, always working.*

Carla: *Me too, you know. In the morning I wake up at six, I wash, and I eat breakfast in a hurry. And how are you?*

Luigi: *I am tired. I never have a moment to enjoy myself.*

Carla: *But at least you have a good job!*

NEW VOCABULARY

addormentarsi	to fall asleep
alzarsi	to get up
a volte	sometimes
di solito	usually
divertirsi	to enjoy oneself
fare colazione	to eat breakfast
finalmente	finally
incontrare	to meet
in fretta	in a hurry
lamentarsi	to complain
lavarsi	to get washed/ to wash oneself
mettersi	to put on
momento	moment
occupato/a	busy
ogni	every
posto	job
riposarsi	to relax
sentirsi	to feel
stanco/a	tired
svegliarsi	to wake up
ufficio	office
uscire	to go out
vestirsi	to get dressed

LESSON 13
CHIEDERE E DARE INDICAZIONI
Asking for and Giving Directions

Signorina Valli:	Scusi, devo andare alla Biblioteca Nazionale. È lontana?
Vigile:	No, può andare a piedi. Alla piazza giri a destra, e poi vada sempre dritto.
Signorina Valli:	Mi può dire anche dov'è il Museo Nazionale Romano?
Vigile:	È vicino. Ritorni indietro e prosegua fino a Piazza della Repubblica.
Signorina Valli:	E per Villa Borghese?
Vigile:	Prenda la metropolitana a Piazza della Repubblica, e scenda a Piazza di Spagna. È la seconda fermata.
Miss Valli:	Pardon me, I have to go to the National Library. Is it far?
Policeman:	No, you can walk there. At the piazza turn right, and then go straight ahead.
Miss Valli:	Can you also tell me where the National Museum of Rome is?
Policeman:	It's very close. Come back and then continue till Piazza della Repubblica.
Miss Valli:	And to the Villa Borghese?
Policeman:	Take the subway at Piazza della Repubblica, and get off at Piazza di Spagna. It's the second stop.

NEW VOCABULARY

accanto	*next to*
a piedi	*by foot*
autobus	*bus*
biblioteca	*library*
chiedere	*to ask*
controllore (m)	*ticket collector*
davanti	*in front of*
destra	*right*
dietro	*behind*
fermata	*stop*
girare	*to turn*
indicazioni	*directions*
lì	*there*
lontano/a	*far*
metropolitana	*subway*
multa	*fine*
proseguire	*to continue*
qui	*here*
ritornare	*to return*
scendere	*to get off*
scusi	*pardon me*
sempre dritto	*straight ahead*
sinistra	*left*
tabaccheria	*tobacco store*
vicino/a	*near*
vigile (m)	*traffic police*

LESSON 14
RADIO E TELEVISIONE
Radio and Television

1.

Lucia:	Metti su Canale 5!
Carlo:	C'è solo una pubblicità.
Lucia:	Abbi pazienza!
Carlo:	Ma cosa c'è?
Lucia:	Non parlare! C'è il concerto di Pavarotti.

Lucia:	Turn to Channel 5!
Carlo:	There is only a commercial.
Lucia:	Be patient!
Carlo:	But what's on?
Lucia:	Don't talk! It's Pavarotti's concert.

2.

Carlo:	Vuole ascoltare un po' di musica alla radio?
Signora Petrini:	Sì, grazie. Accenda la radio!
Carlo:	Ascolti questa canzone!
Signora Petrini:	È carina.

Carlo:	Would you like to listen to some music on the radio?
Mrs. Petrini:	Yes, thank you. Turn on the radio!
Carlo:	Listen to this song!
Mrs. Petrini:	It's nice.

NEW VOCABULARY

accendere	*to turn on*
acoltare	*to listen to*
bambini	*children*
canale (m)	*channel*
canzone (f)	*song*
carino/a	*nice*
cartoni animati	*cartoons*
concerto	*concert*
coraggioso/a	*brave*
gioco a premi	*game show*
guardare	*to watch*
musica	*music*
pazienza	*patience*
pietà	*piety*
pubblicità	*commercial*
radio	*radio*
spegnere	*to turn off*
spesso	*often*
stazione radio (f)	*radio station*
telegiornale (m)	*news*
televisione (f)	*television*

LESSON 15
VIAGGIARE IN TRENO
Traveling by Train

Signor Brizi:	Quand'è il prossimo treno per Milano?
Impiegata:	Sfortunatamente, abbiamo un ritardo di trenta minuti.
Signor Brizi:	Un biglietto di prima classe, per piacere.
Impiegata:	Solo andata?
Signor Brizi:	No, andata e ritorno.
Impiegata:	Va spesso a Milano?
Signor Brizi:	Sì, ci vado regolarmente.
Impiegata:	Ecco a Lei il biglietto!

Mr. Brizi:	When is the next train for Milan?
Clerk:	Unfortunately, it's thirty minutes late.
Mr. Brizi:	A first-class ticket, please.
Clerk:	One-way only?
Mr. Brizi:	No, round-trip.
Clerk:	Do you go to Milan often?
Mr. Brizi:	Yes, I go there regularly.
Clerk:	Here is your ticket!

NEW VOCABULARY

andata e ritorno	*round trip*
biglietteria	*ticket counter*
binario	*track*
cambiare	*to change*
comodamente	*comfortably*
cuccetta	*couchette*
diretto	*express train*
fermarsi	*to stop*
gentilmente	*kindly*
in orario	*on time*
intercity	*rapid train*
locale (m)	*local train*
pendolino	*rapid train*
prima classe (f)	*first class*
prossimo	*next*
quando	*when*
rapido	*rapid train*
recentemente	*recently*
regolarmente	*regularly*
rimanere	*to remain*
ritardo	*delay*
scompartimento	*compartment*
seconda classe (f)	*second class*
sfortunatamente	*unfortunately*
stazione (f)	*station*
stazione ferroviaria (f)	*train station*
supplemento rapido	*additional fee*
treno	*train*
ufficio informazioni	*information desk*
vagone (m)	*car*
vagone ristorante	*dining car*

LESSON 16
IN ALBERGO
In a Hotel

Signora Donati:	Vorrei una camera singola per due notti.
Portiere:	Con bagno? Con doccia?
Signora Donati:	Con bagno, per piacere.
Portiere:	Vuole vedere la camera?
Signora Donati:	Non è necessario. La prendo. Dove posso lasciare le valigie?
Portiere:	Il facchino le porterà in camera.

Mrs. Donati:	I would like a single room for two nights.
Concierge:	With a bathroom? With a shower?
Mrs. Donati:	With a bathroom, please.
Concierge:	Would you like to see the room?
Mrs. Donati:	It's not necessary. I'll take it. Where can I leave my suitcases?
Concierge:	The porter will take them to the room.

NEW VOCABULARY

acqua calda	hot water
albergo	hotel
albergo a due stelle	two-star hotel
bagno	bathroom
camera	room
camera matrimoniale	double room
camera singola	single room
chiave (f)	key
compreso/a	included
doccia	shower
facchino	porter
hotel di prima classe (m)	first-class hotel
lasciare	to leave
necessario/a	necessary
notte (f)	night
ostello	hostel
pagare	to pay
palazzo	palace / building
pensione (f)	family-run hotel
portare	to bring
portiere (m)	concierge
prendere	to take
servizio in camera	room service
sveglia	wake-up call; alarm clock

LESSON 17
UN GIRO IN ITALIA
A Tour in Italy

Signor Carli:	Ci sono giri organizzati dell' Italia meridionale?
Agente di viaggi:	Sì, ma Lei non ha viaggiato con noi l'anno scorso?
Signor Carli:	Sì, sono andato in America un anno fa.
Agente di viaggi:	Quali città ha visitato?
Signor Carli:	Siamo andati a New York e Boston.
Agente di viaggi:	Un bel giro!
Signor Carli:	Sì, ho passato una vacanza favolosa! E quest'anno vorrei fare un giro del mio paese con due miei amici. Non siamo mai stati a sud di Roma.
Agente di viaggi:	Bene, il giro parte da Roma e va a Napoli, in Calabria e in Sicilia.

Mr. Carli:	Are there organized tours of southern Italy?
Travel agent:	Yes, but didn't you already travel with us last year?
Mr. Carli:	Yes, I went to America a year ago.
Travel agent:	Which cities did you visit?
Mr. Carli:	We went to New York and Boston.
Travel agent:	A nice tour!
Mr. Carli:	Yes, I had a fabulous vacation! And this year I'd like to take a tour of my country with two of my friends. We've never been south of Rome.
Travel agent:	Okay, the tour leaves from Rome and goes to Naples, Calabria, and Sicily.

NEW VOCABULARY

agente di viaggi (m/f)	*travel agent*
agenzia di viaggi	*travel agency*
amici	*friends*
cibo	*food*
città	*city*
dialetto	*dialect*
fa	*ago*
giro organizzato	*organized tour*
Italia meridionale	*southern Italy*
itinerario	*itinerary*
meridione (m)	*south*
nord	*north*
paese (m)	*country; town*
pasti	*meals*
scorso/a	*last*
settentrione (m)	*north*
stivale (m)	*boot*
sud	*south*
tariffa	*fare*
tariffa ridotta	*reduced fare*
vacanza	*vacation*
viaggiare	*to travel*
viaggio d'affari	*business trip*
visitare	*to visit*

LESSON 18
UN COLLOQUIO DI LAVORO
A Job Interview

Dott. Jones:	Sono di New York e mi sono laureato in economia e commercio.
Intervistatrice:	Dove ha lavorato, dottore?
Dott. Jones:	A Londra, Madrid, Parigi, sempre nell'industria turistica. Ho sempre voluto lavorare nel settore privato.
Intervistatrice:	Come mai ha deciso di fare domanda?
Dott. Jones:	Nell'annuncio economico ho letto che cercate qualcuno con capacità manageriali.

Dr. Jones:	I'm from New York and I graduated with a degree in business.
Interviewer:	Where have you worked, doctor?
Dr. Jones:	In London, Madrid, Paris, always in the tourism industry. I always wanted to work in the private sector.
Interviewer:	Why did you decide to apply for the job?
Dr. Jones:	In the classified ad I read that you are looking for someone with managerial abilities.

NEW VOCABULARY

aprire	*to open*
annuncio economico	*newspaper ad*
capacità manageriali	*managerial ability*
carriera	*career*
colloquio di lavoro	*job interview*
Come mai?	*How come?*
commercio	*business*
commissione (f)	*commission*
conoscere	*to know*
ditta	*company*
fare domanda	*to apply for a job*
fare le vacanze	*to take a vacation*
industria turistica	*tourism industry*
laurearsi	*to graduate*
lavorare in proprio	*to have one's own business*
lavoro	*job*
morire	*to die*
nascere	*to be born*
orario	*schedule*
prendere le ferie	*to take a vacation*
privato/a	*private*
promozione (f)	*promotion*
qualcuno	*someone*
settore (m)	*sector*
settore dirigenziale (m)	*managerial sector*
stipendio	*salary*
stipendio fisso	*fixed salary*
trovare	*to find*
un bel posto	*a good job*

LESSON 19
GLI SPORT
Sports

Anna:	Mi dai il telecomando, per favore? C'è la partita di calcio.
Marco:	Ma io voglio vedere l'incontro di pugilato.
Anna:	Il pugliato non mi piace. Gli sport violenti non mi piacciono.
Marco:	Il calcio non mi piace affatto.
Anna:	Va bene. Guardiamo invece la partita di pallacanestro.

Anna:	*Would you give me the remote control, please? The soccer game is on.*
Marco:	*But I want to see the boxing match.*
Anna:	*I don't like boxing. I don't like violent sports.*
Marco:	*I don't like soccer at all.*
Anna:	*Okay. Let's watch the basketball game instead.*

NEW VOCABULARY

affatto	*at all*
allenamento	*training*
allenatore (m)	*coach*
calcio	*soccer*
ciclismo	*cycling*
Coppa del Mondo	*World Cup*
giocare	*to play*
giocatore (m)	*player*
incontro	*match*
nuoto	*swimming*
pallacanestro	*basketball*
partita	*game*
perdere	*to lose*
piacere	*to like; to be pleasing*
praticare	*to play (a sport)*
pugilato	*boxing*
sci	*skiing*
scudetto	*championship*
sport	*sport*
squadra	*team*
telecomando	*remote control*
tennis	*tennis*
tifoso	*fan*
vincere	*to win*
violento	*violent*

LESSON 20
LA CASA
The Home

Gina: Hai visto la casa nuova di Rosanna?

Rita: Sì, l'ho vista. È bella, vero?

Gina: Sì, ed è anche molto grande. Ma quante camere da letto ha?

Rita: Ne ha cinque. Ed ha tre bagni e una cucina immensa.

Gina: Sono sicura che per arredarla, ha dovuto comprare molti mobili nuovi.

Gina: *Have you seen Rosanna's new house?*

Rita: *Yes, I saw it. It's beautiful, isn't it?*

Gina: *Yes, and it's also very big. But how many bedrooms does it have?*

Rita: *It has five of them. And it has three bathrooms and a huge kitchen.*

Gina: *I am sure that to furnish it, she had to buy a lot of new furniture.*

NEW VOCABULARY

aria condizionata	*air-conditioning*
armadio a muro	*closet*
arredare	*to furnish*
camera da letto	*bedroom*
casa	*house*
cucina	*kitchen*
divano	*sofa*
diverso/a	*different*
forno	*stove*
frigorifero	*refrigerator*
giardino	*garden*
grande	*big*
ideale	*ideal*
immenso/a	*enormous*
lavapiatti (f)	*dishwasher*
mobili	*furniture*
moquette (f)	*wall-to-wall carpeting*
ne	*some; any; of; about*
nuovo/a	*new*
pianterreno	*ground floor; first floor*
piccolo/a	*small*
primo piano	*second floor*
quadro	*painting*
riscaldamento	*heating*
sala da pranzo	*dining room*
salotto	*living room*
secondo piano	*third floor*
stanza	*room*
tappeto	*area rug*
televisore (m)	*television set*
vecchio/a	*old*

LESSON 21
I GIORNALI
Newspapers

Gianna: C'è qualche notizia interessante?
Sergio: L'editoriale parla del presidente americano.
Gianna: Cosa dice il mio oroscopo?
Sergio: Leone. Farai conoscenze interessanti . . .
          incontrerai un ragazzo alto, bruno,
          gentile . . . vincerai un premio . . . partirai
          per un viaggio.

Gianna: *Is there any interesting news?*
Sergio: *The editorial is about the American president.*
Gianna: *What does my horoscope say?*
Sergio: *Leo. You'll meet interesting people . . . you're
          going to meet a man, tall, dark-haired,
          kind . . . you'll win a prize . . . you'll go on
          a trip.*

NEW VOCABULARY

alto/a	*tall*
articolo	*article*
bruno/a	*brunette*
cronaca mondana	*gossip column*
cultura e spettacoli	*events listing*
edicola	*newsstand*
editoriale (m)	*editorial*
fare conoscenze	*to meet people*
fumetti	*comics*
giornale (m)	*newspaper*
giornalaio	*newspaper vendor*
notizia	*news*
notizie d'attualità	*current events*
notizie internazionali	*international news*
oroscopo	*horoscope*
pagina sportiva	*sports page*
premio	*prize*
qualche	*some*
quotidiano	*local newspaper*
rivista	*magazine*
rubrica finanziaria	*business page*
schedina	*lottery ticket*
settimanale (m)	*weekly magazine*
testata	*headline*

LESSON 22
IN BANCA
At the Bank

Signor Brown:	C'è il dottor Ranieri?
Impiegata:	No, ma c'è il vice direttore, il dottor Miceli.
Signor Brown:	Non lo conosco. Vorrei aprire un conto in banca e depositare dei soldi.
Impiegata:	Ci penso io. Si accomodi allo sportello numero tre. Deve compilare alcuni moduli.

Mr. Brown:	Is Dr. Ranieri in?
Teller:	No, but the assistant manager, Dr. Miceli, is in.
Mr. Brown:	I don't know him. I'd like to open a bank account and deposit some money.
Teller:	I'll take care of it. Please go to window number three. You have to fill out some forms.

NEW VOCABULARY

accomodarsi	to take a place
bancomat	cash/ATM machine
cassa	cashier
compilare	to fill out
conoscere	to know; to be acquainted with
contanti	cash
conto corrente	checking account
conto in banca	bank account
controllare	to check
depositare	to deposit
direttore (m)	manager
dollaro	dollar
modulo	form
prestito	loan
riscuotere	to cash
sapere	to know (a fact)
soldi	money
spiccioli	small change
sportello	window
vice direttore (m)	assistant manager

LESSON 23
L'UFFICIO POSTALE
The Post Office

Franco: Paola, vuoi venire con me all'ufficio postale?
           Devo prendere la pensione della mamma.
           Vorrei fare un telegramma e spedire questo
           pacchetto.

Paola: Anch'io ci devo andare. Devo comprare dei
           francobolli e mandare qualche cartolina.
           Anche Lucia deve imbucare alcune lettere.

Franco: Paola, do you want to come with me to the
           post office? I have to pick up Mom's pension
           check. I'd like to send a telegram, and mail
           this small parcel.

Paola: I have to go there too. I have to buy some
           stamps and mail some postcards. Lucia has
           to mail some letters too.

NEW VOCABULARY

alcuni/e	some
busta	envelope
carta da lettere	writing paper
cartoleria	stationery store
cartolina	postcard
casella postale	mailbox
destinatario	recipient
espresso	express letter
fare un telegramma	to send a telegram
francobolli	stamps
imbucare	to mail
indirizzo	address
lettera	letter
mandare	to send
pacchetto	small parcel
pensione (f)	pension check
per via aerea	air mail
posta	mail
postino	mailman
raccomandata	registered letter
spedire	to send
ufficio postale	post office
un po' di	a bit of

LESSON 24
LA SALUTE
Health

Signora Mancini:	Oggi non sto molto bene: ho la febbre e mi gira la testa.
Dottore:	Sta prendendo delle medicine?
Signora Mancini:	Sì, e sto anche seguendo una cura dimagrante. Non sto mangiando molto.
Dottore:	Prenda queste pasticche tre volte al giorno dopo i pasti.
Signora Mancini:	Occorre la ricetta?
Dottore:	No.

Mrs. Mancini:	I don't feel very well today: I have a fever and I'm dizzy.
Doctor:	Are you taking any medication at the moment?
Mrs. Mancini:	Yes, and I'm also on a diet. I'm not eating much.
Doctor:	Take these pills three times a day after meals.
Mrs. Mancini:	Do I need a prescription?
Doctor:	No.

NEW VOCABULARY

allergico/a	*allergic*
analisi del sangue (m pl)	*blood tests*
cura dimagrante	*diet*
diabete (m)	*diabetes*
fare male	*to hurt*
farsi male	*to get hurt*
febbre (f)	*fever*
girare la testa	*to be dizzy*
malato/a	*sick*
mal di gola	*sore throat*
mal di stomaco	*stomachache*
mal di testa	*headache*
medicina	*medication*
medico	*doctor*
occorrere	*to be necessary*
ospedale	*hospital*
pasticca	*pill; tablet*
paziente (m/f)	*patient*
penicillina	*penicillin*
pressione alta (f)	*high blood pressure*
pressione bassa (m)	*low blood pressure*
Pronto Soccorso	*Emergency Room*
raggi x	*X rays*
ricetta	*prescription*
rompersi	*to break*
rompersi un braccio	*to break an arm*
volta	*time (instance)*

LESSON 25
I COMPUTER E L'INTERNET
Computers and the Internet

1.

Roberto: Voglio ordinare un libro su internet. Ho trovato un buon sito, ma non so come fare un'ordinazione.

Lucia: Dammi il mouse. Guarda. Scegli il libro che vuoi e clicca sulla casella appropriata. Poi riempi il modulo d'ordine con il tuo nome e indirizzo. Ecco fatto!

Roberto: *I want to order a book on the Internet. I found a good site, but I don't know how to place an order.*

Lucia: *Give me the mouse. Watch. First pick the book that you want and click on the right box. Then fill in the order form with your name and address. Done!*

2.

Signora: Ho bisogno di un nuovo modem per il mio computer. Mi faccia vedere quel modello in vetrina, per favore. È un buon modello?

Impiegato: Sappia che questo è l'ultimo modello sul mercato.

Signora: Va bene, lo prendo.

Woman: *I need a new modem for my computer. Let me see that model in the window, please. Is it a good model?*

Clerk: *You can be assured that this is the latest model on the market.*

Woman: *Okay, I'll take it.*

NEW VOCABULARY

acquistare in linea	to purchase online
battere	to type
casella	box (on the computer screen)
cliccare	to click
collegarsi a un sito	to connect to a Web site
computer (m)	computer
controllare	to check
cursore (m)	cursor
dischetto	disk
e-mail (m)	e-mail
fare un'ordinazione	to place an order
homepage (f)	home page
indirizzo e-mail	e-mail address
internet (m)	Internet
link (m)	link
modem (m)	modem
mouse (m)	mouse
navigare la rete	to surf the Net
navigare su internet	to surf the Internet
posta elettronica	e-mail (in general)
rete (f)	Internet
schermo	monitor
scegliere	to choose
sito	Web site
software (m)	software
stampante (f)	printer
stampante laser (f)	laser printer
stampare	to print
tastiera	keyboard
unità	drive
utente (m/f)	user

LESSON 26
ALL'OPERA
To the Opera

Mario: Che film davano ieri?

Giulia: Un film di Fellini.

Mario: Volevo venire, ma non ho potuto. Carla voleva andare all'opera. Mentre aspettavamo in fila per i biglietti, è cominciato a piovere. E quando siamo arrivati al botteghino, non riuscivo a trovare i soldi.

Giulia: E lo spettacolo?

Mario: Fantastica la messinscena, bravissimi i cantanti.

Mario: *What movie were they showing yesterday?*

Giulia: *A film by Fellini.*

Mario: *I wanted to come, but I couldn't. Carla wanted to go to the opera. While we were waiting in line for the tickets, it started to rain. And when we got to the ticket booth, I couldn't find the money.*

Giulia: *And the show?*

Mario: *The staging was fantastic, the singers were excellent.*

NEW VOCABULARY

applaudire	to applaud
assistere ad uno spettacolo	to go to a show
attore	actor
attrice	actress
balletto	ballet
botteghino	ticket booth
bravissimo/a	wonderful
commedia	comedy
dramma (m)	drama
fila	line
iniziare	to begin
mentre	while
messinscena	staging
opera	opera
ottimista (m/f)	optimistic
palcoscenico	stage
parte (f)	part
pessimista (m/f)	pessimistic
preferito/a	favorite
protagonista (m/f)	protagonist
regista (m/f)	director
riuscire	to succeed
sipario	curtain
stupendo/a	wonderful
tenore (m)	tenor
tragedia	tragedy
trama	plot

LESSON 27
LA MUSICA
Music

Antonio:	Sono andato a vedere il concerto di Claudio Baglioni.
Mary:	Davvero? È il mio cantante preferito. Eri mai stato ad un suo concerto prima?
Antonio:	Si, c'ero già andato due anni fa. La sua musica, però, è un po' cambiata.
Mary:	L'avevo già notato nel suo ultimo CD, ma mi piace molto quella nuova canzone.

Antonio:	I went to see Claudio Baglioni's concert.
Mary:	Really? He's my favorite singer. Had you ever been to one of his concerts before?
Antonio:	Yes, I had already gone to one two years ago. But his music has changed a bit.
Mary:	I had already noticed that in his latest CD, but I really like that new song.

NEW VOCABULARY

ballare	*to dance*
cantante (m/f)	*singer*
cantautore (m)	*singer-songwriter*
cantautrice (f)	*songwriter*
complesso musicale	*music group*
concedere un bis	*to give an encore*
concerto all'aperto	*open-air concert*
fare una tournée	*to go on tour*
festival della canzone (m)	*song festival*
già	*already*
musicista (m/f)	*musician*
notare	*to notice*
pubblico	*audience*

LESSON 28
FRUTTA E VERDURA
Fruits and Vegetables

Fruttivendolo:	Frutta! Verdura! La roba più fresca del mondo! Signora, guardi queste fragole!
Signora Marini:	Le ciliege mi sembrano più buone delle fragole. Quanto costano?
Fruttivendolo:	Tre euro al chilo. Alla bancarella di fronte sono più care.
Signora Marini:	Troppo!
Fruttivendolo:	Le mele e le arance però sono meno costose, ma sono molto buone.
Signora Marini:	Va bene, compro due chili di mele.

Fruit seller:	Fruit! Vegetables! The freshest stuff in the world! Madam, look at these strawberries!
Mrs. Marini:	The cherries seem better than the strawberries. How much do they cost?
Fruit seller:	Three euros a kilo. At the stand in front they are more expensive.
Mrs. Marini:	Too much!
Fruit seller:	The apples and oranges though are less expensive, but they're very good.
Mrs. Marini:	Okay, I'll buy two kilos of apples.

NEW VOCABULARY

anguria	*watermelon*
arancia	*orange*
assai	*quite*
bancarella	*fruit stand*
carota	*carrot*
cetriolo	*cucumber*
chilo	*kilo*
ciliegia	*cherry*
cipolla	*onion*
così	*as*
costoso/a	*expensive*
dolce	*sweet*
fagiolini (m pl)	*string beans*
fico	*fig*
fragola	*strawberry*
fresco/a	*fresh*
frutta	*fruit*
fruttivendolo	*fruit seller*
lattuga	*lettuce*
limone (m)	*lemon*
mela	*apple*
melanzana	*eggplant*
melone (m)	*melon*
meno	*less*
mercato	*open-air market*
mercato delle pulci	*flea market*
patata	*potato*
peperone (m)	*bell pepper*
pera	*pear*
pesca	*peach*
piselli (m pl)	*peas*
più	*more*
roba	*produce*
spinaci (m pl)	*spinach*
uva	*grapes*

LESSON 29
AL SUPERMERCATO
At the Supermarket

Daniele:	Maria, che cosa ci serve?
Maria:	La pasta, il sale, l'olio, l'aceto, un po' di carne, della senape, del ketchup, del miele.
Daniele:	Ci servono degli affettati?
Maria:	Sì, cinquecento grammi di mortadella.
Daniele:	Quale vino vuoi comprare?
Maria:	Del vino italiano, è il migliore del mondo.
Daniele:	Anche quello francese è ottimo.
Maria:	Andiamo alla cassa.

Daniele:	*Maria, what do we need?*
Maria:	*Pasta, salt, oil, vinegar, some meat, mustard, ketchup, honey.*
Daniele:	*Do we need cold cuts?*
Maria:	*Yes, five hundred grams of mortadella.*
Daniele:	*Which wine do you want to buy?*
Maria:	*Some Italian wine, it's the best in the world.*
Daniele:	*French wine is excellent as well.*
Maria:	*Let's go to the checkout.*

NEW VOCABULARY

aceto	*vinegar*
affettare	*to slice*
affettati (m pl)	*cold cuts*
bene	*well*
buono/a	*good*
burro	*butter*
carta igienica	*toilet paper*
cassa	*cash register*
cattivo/a	*bad*
chilo	*kilo*
Cosa ci serve?	*What do we need?*
dado di manzo	*beef bouillon*
dentifricio	*toothpaste*
dozzina	*dozen*
fare la spesa	*to go grocery shopping*
grande (m/f)	*big; great*
latte (m)	*milk*
lista della spesa	*shopping list*
maggiore	*bigger; greater; older*
male	*badly*
marmellata	*jam*
meglio (adv)	*better*
miele (m)	*honey*
migliore	*better*
minore	*smaller; younger*
olio	*oil*
pane (m)	*bread*
peggio (adv)	*worse*
peggiore	*worse*
pepe (m)	*pepper*
piccolo/a	*small*
sale (m)	*salt*
senape (f)	*mustard*
servire	*to need*
sottile	*thin*
supermercato	*supermarket*
surgelati	*frozen foods*
uova (f pl)	*eggs*
zucchero	*sugar*

LESSON 30
ALLA TABACCHERIA
At the Tobacco Store

Mark:	Un pacchetto di Nazionali, per favore. Qui si vendono biglietti per l'autobus?
Tabaccaia:	Sì, i biglietti si comprano qui. Quanti ne vuole?
Mark:	Solamente uno. Dove si può trovare della carta da lettere?
Tabaccaia:	Anche qui si vende la carta da lettere. Qui in Italia si vende un po' di tutto nelle tabaccherie. Si possono comprare sigarette, francobolli, cartoline, articoli da regalo.

Mark:	A pack of Nazionali, please. Do you sell bus tickets here?
Tobacconist:	Yes, tickets are bought here. How many would you like?
Mark:	Just one. Where can I find some writing paper?
Tobacconist:	We also sell writing paper. Here in Italy we sell a little bit of everything in tobacco shops. You can buy cigarettes, stamps, postcards, gift items.

NEW VOCABULARY

accendino	*lighter*
articoli da regalo	*gift items*
caramelle	*candy*
fiammiferi	*matches*
fumare	*to smoke*
gomma americana	*chewing gum*
pacchetto	*pack*
pipa	*pipe*
ricordo	*souvenir*
rullino	*roll of film*
rullino da 24 pose	*24-exposure roll of film*
sigarette	*cigarettes*
soltanto	*only*
stecca di sigarette	*carton of cigarettes*
tabaccheria	*tobacco store*
un po' di tutto	*a little bit of everything*
zona fumatori	*smoking section*

LESSON 31
I CAPELLI
Hair

1.

Gino: Mi taglieresti i capelli?
Mamma: Certo, come li vuoi?
Gino: Vorrei solo una spuntatina.
Mamma: Perchè non li porti più corti? Io sarei più contenta!
Gino: No, li preferisco lunghi.
Mamma: Come vuoi tu!

Gino: *Would you cut my hair?*
Mother: *Sure, how would you like it cut?*
Gino: *I'd just like a trim.*
Mother: *Why don't you keep it shorter? I would be happier!*
Gino: *No, I prefer it long.*
Mother: *Whatever you like!*

2.

Signora Carli: Vorrei tingermi i capelli biondi.
Parrucchière: Le suggerirei questa tintura.
Signora Carli: Ne avrebbe una più scura?
Parrucchière: Ecco!

Mrs. Carli: *I'd like to dye my hair blond.*
Hairdresser: *I'd suggest this shade.*
Mrs. Carli: *Would you have a darker one?*
Hairdresser: *Here we are!*

NEW VOCABULARY

barbiere (m)	*barber*
biondo/a	*blond*
capelli	*hair*
corto/a	*short*
farsi la barba	*to shave*
lacca	*hairspray*
lato	*side*
liscio/a	*straight*
lunghezza	*length*
lungo/a	*long*
ondulato/a	*wavy*
parrucchière (m)	*beauty parlor; hairdresser*
permanente (f)	*permanent*
riccio/a	*curly*
salone (m)	*salon*
scuro/a	*dark*
spuntatina	*trim*
suggerire	*to suggest*
tagliare	*to cut*
tingere	*to dye*
tintura	*shade*

LESSON 32
I SOLDI
Money

Signorina Meli:	Vorrei cambiare questi dollari in euro, per piacere. Quanto è il cambio oggi?
Signor Risi:	Beh, oggi non è molto alto. Li vorrebbe in contanti?
Signorina Meli:	Si, potrei anche cambiare questo traveler's check?
Signor Risi:	Come no!
Miss Meli:	*I'd like to exchange these dollars into euros, please. What's the exchange rate today?*
Mr. Risi:	*Well, it's not very high today. Would you like it in cash?*
Miss Meli:	*Yes, could I also change this traveler's check?*
Mr. Risi:	*Of course!*

NEW VOCABULARY

alto/a	*high*
assegno	*check*
basso/a	*low*
cambio *(money)*	*exchange rate*
come no	*of course*
firmare	*to sign*
listino dei cambi	*exchange list*
sportello dei cambi	*exchange window*
tassa del cambio	*exchange rate*
totale (m)	*total*
ufficio del cambio	*currency exchange office*

LESSON 33
NOLEGGIARE UNA MACCHINA
Renting a Car

Signora Smith:	Vorrei noleggiare una macchina con il cambio automatico.
Impiegato:	Le macchine con il cambio automatico sono tutte esurite.
Signora Smith:	Ma l'ho ordinata un mese fa!
Impiegato:	L'avrebbe dovuta ordinare prima.
Signora Smith:	L'avrei ordinata prima, ma non ho potuto.

Mrs. Smith:	I'd like to rent a car with an automatic gear shift.
Clerk:	The automatic cars have all been rented out.
Mrs. Smith:	But I reserved it a month ago!
Clerk:	You should have reserved it earlier.
Mrs. Smith:	I would have reserved it earlier, but I couldn't.

NEW VOCABULARY

assicurazione (f)	*insurance*
cambio *(car)*	*gear shift (car)*
cambio automatico	*automatic gear shift*
esaurito/a	*rented out*
incluso/a	*included*
macchina con le marce	*a stick-shift car*
noleggiare	*to rent*
noleggio	*rental*
pagamento anticipato	*advance payment*
patente (f)	*license*
portabagagli (m)	*trunk*
prima	*earlier*
pulmino	*minivan*
registrazione (f)	*registration*
tipo	*type*
utilitaria	*compact car*

LESSON 34
IN UN NEGOZIO DI SCARPE
In a Shoe Store

Cliente:	Vorrei un paio di scarpe.
Commessa:	Che numero porta?
Cliente:	Non sono sicura.
Commessa:	Penso che Lei porti il trentasette. Provi queste.
Cliente:	Mi stanno strette.
Commessa:	E queste?
Cliente:	Mi stanno bene. Spero che non costino troppo.

Client:	I'd like a pair of shoes.
Salesperson:	What size do you wear?
Client:	I am not sure.
Salesperson:	I think you wear a thirty-seven. Try these on.
Client:	They're tight.
Salesperson:	And these?
Client:	They fit well. I hope they don't cost too much.

NEW VOCABULARY

comodo/a	comfortable
credere	to believe
cuoio	leather
desiderare	to desire
dubitare	to doubt
fatto a mano	handmade
largo/a	big
numero	size
paio	pair
pensare	to think
qualcosa di meno caro	something less expensive
sandali	sandals
scarpe	shoes
scarpe da donna	women's shoes
scarpe da tennis	tennis shoes
scarpe da uomo	men's shoes
sicuro/a	certain; sure
sperare	to hope
stivali	boots
stretto/a	tight
suola	shoe sole
tacchi alti/bassi	high/low heels

LESSON 35
UN GIRO DELLA CITTÀ
A Tour of the City

Turista:	Ha una pianta della città?
Impiegato:	Sì, ecco.
Turista:	Vorrei vedere qualche museo, però dubito che siano aperti.
Impiegato:	Oggi è lunedì. Sono sicuro che i musei sono chiusi.
Turista:	Spero che ci siano delle manifestazioni questa settimana.
Impiegato:	Penso che domani ci sia una mostra di fiori.

Tourist:	Do you have a map of the city?
Clerk:	Yes, here you are.
Tourist:	I'd like to see some museums, but I doubt they are open.
Clerk:	Today is Monday. I am sure the museums are closed.
Tourist:	I hope that there are some special events this week.
Clerk:	I think that tomorrow there is a flower show.

NEW VOCABULARY

aperto/a	*open*
carnevale (m)	*carnival*
carta geografica	*map*
centro commerciale	*commercial center*
centro storico	*historic center*
chiesa	*church*
chiuso/a	*closed*
elenco	*list*
È meglio che . . .	*It's better that . . .*
È necessario che . . .	*It's necessary that . . .*
È possibile che . . .	*It's possible that . . .*
fiori	*flowers*
guida turistica	*guidebook*
manifestazione (f)	*special event*
mostra	*show*
museo	*museum*
pianta	*map*
straniero/a	*foreigner*
ufficio informazioni turistiche	*tourist information office*
zona	*zone*

GRAMMAR SUMMARY

1. Subject Pronouns

io	*I*
tu	*you (infml)*
lui	*he*
lei	*she*
Lei	*you (fml)*
noi	*we*
voi	*you (pl)*
loro	*they*

2. Emphatic Pronouns

me	*me*
te	*you (infml)*
lui	*him*
lei	*her*
Lei	*you (fml)*
noi	*us*
voi	*you (pl)*
loro	*them*

3. Reflexive Pronouns

mi	*myself*
ti	*yourself (infml)*
si	*him/her/it/oneself*
Si	*yourself (fml)*
ci	*ourselves*
vi	*yourselves*
si	*themselves*
Si	*yourselves (fml)*

4. Direct Object Pronouns

mi	*me*
ti	*you (infml)*
lo	*him, it (m)*
la	*her, it (f)*
La	*you (fml)*
ci	*us*
vi	*you (pl)*
li	*them (m)*
le	*them (f)*

5. Indirect Object Pronouns

mi	*to me*
ti	*to you (infml)*
gli	*to him, to it (m)*
le	*to her, to it (f)*
Le	*to you (fml)*
ci	*to us*
vi	*to you (pl)*
gli	*to them*

6. Double Object Pronouns

	+LO	+LA	+LI	+LE	+NE
MI	me lo	me la	me li	me le	me ne
TI	te lo	te la	te li	te le	te ne
GLI/LE/LE	glielo	gliela	glieli	gliele	gliene
CI	ce lo	ce la	ce li	ce le	ce ne
VI	ve lo	ve la	ve li	ve le	ve ne
GLI	glielo	gliela	glieli	gliele	gliene

75

7. Plural of Nouns and Adjectives

	SINGULAR	PLURAL
MASCULINE	-o	-i
MASC./FEM.	-e	-i
FEMININE	-a	-e

8. Indefinite Articles (A, An)

	MASC.	FEM.
BEFORE . . .		
A CONSONANT	un	un
S+CONSONANT OR Z	uno	una
A VOWEL	un	un'

9. Definite Articles (The)

MASCULINE	SINGULAR	PLURAL
BEFORE . . .		
A CONSONANT	il	i
S+CONSONANT OR Z	lo	gli
A VOWEL	l'	gli

FEMININE	SINGULAR	PLURAL
BEFORE . . .		
A CONSONANT	la	le
A VOWEL	l'	le

10. Prepositions + Definite Articles

SINGULAR

	+LO	+L'	+IL	+LA
DI	dello	dell'	del	della
A	allo	all'	al	alla
DA	dallo	dall'	dal	dalla
IN	nello	nell'	nel	nella
SU	sullo	sull'	sul	sulla

PLURAL

	+GLI	+I	+LE
DI	degli	dei	delle
A	agli	ai	alle
DA	dagli	dai	dalle
IN	negli	nei	nelle
SU	sugli	sui	sulle

11. Demonstrative Pronouns

A. THIS ONE/THESE

	SINGULAR	PLURAL
MASCULINE	questo	questi
FEMININE	questa	queste

B. THAT ONE/THOSE

	SINGULAR	PLURAL
MASCULINE	quello	quelli
FEMININE	quella	quelle

12. Demonstrative Adjectives

A. THIS ONE/THESE

	SINGULAR	PLURAL
MASCULINE	questo	questi
FEMININE	questa	queste

B. THAT/THOSE

MASCULINE	SINGULAR	PLURAL
BEFORE . . .		
A CONSONANT	quel	quei
S+CONSONANT OR Z	quello	quegli
A VOWEL	quell'	quegli

FEMININE	SINGULAR	PLURAL
BEFORE . . .		
A CONSONANT	quella	quelle
A VOWEL	quell'	quelle

13. Possessive Adjectives

MASCULINE

SINGULAR	PLURAL	
il mio	i miei	*my*
il tuo	i tuoi	*your (infml)*
il suo	i suoi	*his/her/its*
il Suo	i Suoi	*your (fml)*
il nostro	i nostri	*our*
il vostro	i vostri	*your (pl)*
il loro	i loro	*their*

FEMININE

SINGULAR	PLURAL	
la mia	le mie	*my*
la tua	le tue	*your (infml)*
la sua	le sue	*his/her/its*
la Sua	le Sue	*your (fml)*
la nostra	le nostre	*our*
la vostra	le vostre	*your (pl)*
la loro	le loro	*their*

14. Comparatives

piu . . . di/che	*more . . . than*
meno . . . di/che	*less . . . than*
così . . . come	*as . . . as*
tanto . . . quanto	*as much . . . as*

15. Irregular Comparatives and Superlatives

buono/a →	migliore →	il/la migliore
good →	*better* →	*the best*
cattivo/a →	peggiore →	il/la peggiore
bad →	*worse* →	*the worst*
grande →	maggiore →	il/la maggiore
big →	*bigger* →	*the biggest*
great →	*greater* →	*the greatest*
piccolo/a →	minore →	il/la minore
small →	*smaller* →	*smallest*

ottimo	*very good*
pessimo	*very bad*
massimo	*very big / very great*
minimo	*very small*

16. The Adjective *Bello* (Beautiful)

Bello usually precedes the noun, and its forms resemble those of the definite articles:

	MASCULINE	
	SINGULAR	PLURAL
BEFORE . . .		
A CONSONANT	bel	bei
S+CONSONANT		
OR Z	bello	begli
A VOWEL	bell'	begli

	FEMININE	
	SINGULAR	PLURAL
BEFORE . . .		
A CONSONANT	bella	belle
A VOWEL	bell'	belle

Bello can follow a noun for emphasis, in which case it has the following forms:

	SINGULAR	PLURAL
MASCULINE	bello	belli
FEMININE	bella	belle

17. The Adjective *Buono* (Good)

When buono follows the noun, it has the following four forms:

	SINGULAR	PLURAL
MASCULINE	buono	buoni
FEMININE	buona	buone

When buono precedes the noun, the singular forms resemble those of the indefinite articles:

	MASC.	FEM.
BEFORE . . .		
A CONSONANT	buon	buona
S+CONSONANT		
OR Z	buono	buona
A VOWEL	buon	buon'

18. Double Negatives

non . . . più	no more/longer
non . . . ancora	not yet
non . . . affatto	not at all
non . . . niente/nulla	nothing
non . . . nessuno	no one
non . . . mai	never
non . . . né . . . né	neither . . . nor

19. Regular Verbs Ending in -ARE

	io	noi
	tu	voi
	lui / lei / Lei	loro / Loro

INDICTIVE

Present		Present Perfect	
-o	-iamo	ho/sono + p.p.	abbiamo/siamo + p.p.
-i	-ate	hai/sei + p.p.	avete/siete + p.p.
-a	-ano	ha/è + p.p.	hanno/sono + p.p.

Imperfect		Past Perfect	
-vo	-vamo	avevo/ero + p.p.	avevamo/eravamo + p.p.
-vi	-vate	avevi/eri + p.p.	avevate/eravate + p.p.
-va	-vano	aveva/era + p.p.	avevano/erano + p.p.

Absolute Past		Preterite Perfect	
-ai	-ammo	ebbi/fui + p.p.	avemmo/fummo + p.p.
-asti	-aste	avesti/fosti + p.p.	aveste/foste + p.p.
-ò	-arono	ebbe/fu + p.p.	ebbero/furono + p.p.

Future		Future Perfect	
-ò	-emo	avrò/sarò + p.p.	avremo/saremo + p.p.
-ai	-ete	avrai/sarai + p.p.	avrete/sarete + p.p.
-à	-anno	avrà/sarà + p.p.	avranno/saranno + p.p.

SUBJUNCTIVE

Present		Past	
-i	-iamo	abbia/sia + p.p.	abbiamo/siamo + p.p.
-i	-iate	abbia/sia + p.p.	abbiate/siate + p.p.
-i	-ino	abbia/sia + p.p.	abbiano/siano + p.p.

Imperfect		Past Perfect	
-assi	-assimo	avessi/fossi + p.p.	avessimo/fossimo + p.p.
-assi	-aste	avessi/fossi + p.p.	aveste/foste + p.p.
-asse	-assero	avesse/fosse + p.p.	avessero/fossero + p.p.

CONDITIONAL

Present		Past	
-ei	-emmo	avrei/sarei + p.p.	avremmo/saremmo + p.p.
-esti	-este	avresti/saresti + p.p.	avreste/sareste + p.p.
-ebbe	-ebbero	avrebbe/sarebbe + p.p.	avrebbero/sarebbero + p.p.

Imperative		Participles	Gerund
	-iamo	**Present**	-ando
-a	-ate	-ante	
-i	-ino	**Past**	
		-ato	

20. Regular Verbs Ending in -*ERE*

INDICATIVE

Present		**Present Perfect**	
-o	-iamo	ho/sono + p.p.	abbiamo/siamo + p.p.
-i	-ete	hai/sei + p.p.	avete/siete + p.p.
-e	-ono	ha/è + p.p.	hanno/sono + p.p.

Imperfect		**Past Perfect**	
-vo	-vamo	avevo/ero + p.p.	avevamo/eravamo + p.p.
-vi	-vate	avevi/eri + p.p.	avevate/eravate + p.p.
-va	-vano	aveva/era + p.p.	avevano/erano + p.p.

Absolute Past		**Preterite Perfect**	
-ei (-etti)	-emmo	ebbi/fui + p.p.	avemmo/fummo + p.p.
-esti	-este	avesti/fosti + p.p.	aveste/foste + p.p.
-è (-ette)	-erono (-ettero)	ebbe/fu + p.p.	ebbero/furono + p.p.

Future		**Future Perfect**	
-ò	-emo	avrò/sarò + p.p.	avremo/saremo + p.p.
-ai	-ete	avrai/sarai + p.p.	avrete/sarete + p.p.
-à	-anno	avrà/sarà + p.p.	avranno/saranno + p.p.

SUBJUNCTIVE

Present		**Past**	
-a	-iamo	abbia/sia + p.p.	abbiamo/siamo + p.p.
-a	-iate	abbia/sia + p.p.	abbiate/siate + p.p.
-a	-ano	abbia/sia + p.p.	abbiano/siano + p.p.

Imperfect		**Past Perfect**	
-essi	-essimo	avessi/fossi + p.p.	avessimo/fossimo + p.p.
-essi	-este	avessi/fossi + p.p.	aveste/foste + p.p.
-esse	-essero	avesse/fosse + p.p.	avessero/fossero + p.p.

CONDITIONAL

Present		**Past**	
-ei	-emmo	avrei/sarei + p.p.	avremmo/saremmo + p.p.
-esti	-este	avresti/saresti + p.p.	avreste/sareste + p.p.
-ebbe	-ebbero	avrebbe/sarebbe + p.p.	avrebbero/sarebbero + p.p.

IMPERATIVE

—	-iamo
-i	-ete
-a	-ono

PARTICIPLES

Present
-ente

Past
-uto

GERUND

-endo

21. Regular Verbs Ending in -*IRE*

INDICATIVE

Present		Present Perfect	
-o/-isco	-iamo	ho/sono + p.p.	abbiamo/siamo + p.p.
-i/-isci	-ite	hai/sei + p.p.	avete/siete + p.p.
-e/-isce	-ono/-iscono	ha/è + p.p.	hanno/sono + p.p.

Imperfect		Past Perfect	
-vo	-vamo	avevo/ero + p.p.	avevamo/eravamo + p.p.
-vi	-vate	avevi/eri + p.p.	avevate/eravate + p.p.
-va	-vano	aveva/era + p.p.	avevano/erano + p.p.

Absolute Past		Preterite Perfect	
-ii	-immo	ebbi/fui + p.p.	avemmo/fummo + p.p.
-isti	-iste	avesti/fosti + p.p.	aveste/foste + p.p.
-i	-irono	ebbe/fu + p.p.	ebbero/furono + p.p.

Future		Future Perfect	
-ò	-emo	avrò/sarò + p.p.	avremo/saremo + p.p.
-ai	-ete	avrai/sarai + p.p.	avrete/sarete + p.p.
-à	-anno	avrà/sarà + p.p.	avranno/saranno + p.p.

SUBJUNCTIVE

Present		Past	
-a/-isca	-iamo	abbia/sia + p.p.	abbiamo/siamo + p.p.
-a/-isca	-iate	abbia/sia + p.p.	abbiate/siate + p.p.
-a/-isca	-ano/-iscano	abbia/sia + p.p.	abbiano/siano + p.p.

Imperfect		Past Perfect	
-issi	-issimo	avessi/fossi + p.p.	avessimo/fossimo + p.p.
-issi	-iste	avessi/fossi + p.p.	aveste/foste + p.p.
-isse	-issero	avesse/fosse + p.p.	avessero/fossero + p.p.

CONDITIONAL

Present	Past		
-ei	-emmo	avrei/sarei + p.p.	avremmo/saremmo + p.p.
-esti	-este	avresti/saresti + p.p.	avreste/sareste + p.p.
-ebbe	-ebbero	avrebbe/sarebbe + p.p.	avrebbero/sarebbero + p.p.

IMPERATIVE

——	-iamo
-i	-ite
-a	-ano

PARTICIPLES

Present
-ente

Past
-ito

GERUND

-endo

GLOSSARY OF GRAMMATICAL TERMS

active voice—forma attiva: *a verbal form in which the agent of an action is expressed as the grammatical subject; e.g.,* Tutti leggono questo libro. *(Everyone is reading this book.)*

adjective—aggettivo: *a word that describes a noun; e.g.,* grande *(large).*

adverb—avverbio: *a word that describes verbs, adjectives, or other adverbs; e.g.,* rapidamente *(quickly).*

agreement—accordo: *the modification of a word according to the person, gender, or number of another word which it describes or to which it relates; e.g.,* il ragazzo alto *(m),* la ragazza alta *(f).*

auxiliary verb—verbo ausiliare: *a helping verb used with another verb to express some facet of tense or mood, e.g.,* avere *(to have).*

compound—composto: *when used in reference to verbal forms, it indicates a tense composed of two parts: an auxiliary and a main verb. For example:* Ho dormito *(I slept).*

conditional—condizionale: *the mood used for hypothetical (depending on a possible condition or circumstance) statements and questions; e.g.,* lo mangerei se . . . *(I would eat if . . .).*

conjugation—coniugazione: *the modification of a verb according to person and tense or mood.*

conjunction—congiunzione: *a word that connects words and phrases; e.g.,* e *(and),* ma *(but), etc.*

definite article—articolo determinativo: *a word linked to a noun; generally used to indicate the noun is a specific instance of a general category. In Italian, the definite articles (meaning "the") are:* il, lo, i, gli, la, le.

demonstrative—dimostrativo: *a word used to indicate the position of a noun in relation to the speaker. Demonstrative adjectives are used together* with a noun (Mi piace questa città.—*I like this city.*), and demonstrative pronouns replace the noun (Mi piace questa.—*I like this one.*).

direct object—oggetto diretto: *the person or thing undergoing the action of a verb. For example, in the sentence "I wrote a letter to John," the direct object is "a letter."*

ending—desinenza: *the suffixes added to the stem that indicate gender, number, tense, mood, or part of speech.*

gender—genere: *grammatical categories for nouns, generally unrelated to physical gender and often determined by word ending. Italian has two genders—masculine and feminine—which refer to both animate and inanimate nouns; e.g., il fiume (m), la città (f).*

gerund—gerundio: *In Italian, an invariable verbal form which always appears in dependent clauses and expresses an action taking place simultaneously with that of the main verb. Used to form the present and past progressive; e.g., sto scherzando (I'm joking), stavo scherzando (I was joking).*

imperative—imperativo: *the command form; e.g., Fai attenzione! (Pay attention!).*

imperfect—imperfetto: *the past tense used to describe ongoing or habitual actions or states without a specified time frame; often referred to as the descriptive past tense.*

impersonal verb—verbo impersonale: *a verb lacking a real subject; always used in the third person. In English, the subject of impersonal verbs is usually "it." Impersonal verbs are often used to indicate natural phenomena, such as weather, climate, or time (Fa freddo in inverno.—It's cold in winter.), as well as in various set expressions such as occorre che . . . (It's necessary that . . .), È vero che . . . (It's true that . . .), etc.*

indefinite article—articolo indeterminativo: *a word linked to a noun; used when referring to a noun or class of nouns in a general way. In Italian the indefinite articles (meaning "a, an") are: un, una, uno.*

indicative—indicativo: *the mood used for factual or objective statements and questions.*

indirect object—oggetto indiretto: *the ultimate recipient of the action of a verb; often introduced by a preposition. For example, in the sentence "I wrote a letter to John," the indirect object is "John."*

infinitive—infinito: *the basic, uninflected form of a verb found in the dictionary, i.e., before the person, number, tense, or mood have been specified; e.g., parlare (to speak).*

intransitive—intransitivo: *a verb which may not take a direct object.*

inversion—inversione: *reversing the order of subject and verb, often used in question formation.*

mood—modo: *a reflection of the speaker's attitude toward what is expressed by the verb. The major moods in Italian are the Indicative, the Subjunctive, and the Imperative.*

noun—nome: *a word referring to a person, place, thing, or abstract idea; e.g., città (city), amore (love), etc.*

number—numero: *the distinction between singular and plural.*

participle—participio: *a verbal form that often has the function of an adjective or adverb but may have the verbal features of tense and voice; often used in the formation of compound tenses, e.g., present and past participles: passante/passato (passing/passed).*

passive voice—forma passiva: *a verbal form in which the recipient of the action is expressed as the grammatical subject; e.g., Questo libro è letto da tutti. (This book is read by everyone.)*

person—persona: *the grammatical category that distinguishes between the speaker (first person—I, we), the person spoken to (second person—you), and the people and things spoken about (third person—he, she, it, they). It is often used in reference to pronouns and verbs.*

pluperfect—passato anteriore: *the past perfect.*

possessive—possessivo: *indicating ownership; e.g., mio (my) is a possessive adjective.*

predicate—predicato: the part of a clause that expresses the state of the subject; it usually contains the verb with or without objects and complements.

preposition—preposizione: a word used to express spatial, temporal, or other relationships; e.g., a (to), su (on), etc.

present perfect—passato prossimo: the past tense used to describe actions that began and were completed in the past, usually at a single moment or during a specific period; useful for narration of events.

pronoun—pronome: a word that replaces a noun; e.g., io (I), lo (him/it), questo (this).

reflexive verb—verbo riflessivo: a verb conjugated with a pronoun in addition to the subject. Reflexive verbs can express action which reflects back on the subject (Mi lavo la faccia.—I am washing my face.) or which is reciprocal (Ci siamo incontrati ieri.—We met each other yesterday.).

simple—semplice: one-word verbal forms conjugated by adding endings to a stem.

stem—radice: in conjugation, the part of a verb used as the base to which endings are added. The stem used to form most simple tenses of Italian regular verbs is derived by simply dropping the infinitive ending (-are, -ire, -ere); e.g., parlare → parl- → io parlo.

subject—soggetto: the agent of an action or the entity experiencing the state described by a verb. For example, in the sentence "I wrote a letter to John," the subject is "I."

subjunctive—congiuntivo: the mood used for nonfactual or subjective statements or questions.

tense—tempo: the time of an action or state, i.e., past, present, future.

transitive—transitivo: a verb which may take a direct object.

verb—verbo: a word expressing an action or state; e.g., scrivere (to write).